Journal Your Way to LOVE

Find Acceptance When All You Feel Is Rejected

MATT PAVLIK

BRINGING YOUR POTENTIAL TO LIGHT

Christian Concepts
Centerville, Ohio

Journal Your Way To Love
Copyright © 2020 by Matt Pavlik.

All rights reserved. No part of this book may be used or reproduced in any manner whatsoever without written permission except in the case of brief quotations embodied in critical articles or reviews.

Published in the United States of America by Christian Concepts (christianconcepts.com), an imprint of New Reflections Counseling, Inc. (newreflectionscounseling.com).

Although the author is a professional counselor, this book is not intended to be a replacement for professional counseling.

First Edition: December 2020

REL012150 RELIGION / Christian Living / Devotional Journal

Pavlik, Matthew Edward, 1971-
Journal Your Way To Love / Matt Pavlik.

ISBN: 978-1-951866-03-7 (softcover)

1. Spiritual journals—Authorship—Religious aspects—Christianity
2. Diaries—Authorship—Religious aspects—Christianity

Journaling, Love, Healing, Growth, Self-acceptance, Meaning (Philosophy), Rejection (Psychology), Self-deception

Scripture quotations marked NLT are taken from the Holy Bible, New Living Translation, copyright © 1996, 2004, 2015 by Tyndale House Foundation. Used by permission of Tyndale House Publishers, Inc., Carol Stream, Illinois 60188. All rights reserved.

Scripture quotations marked (NIV) are taken from the Holy Bible, New International Version®, NIV®. Copyright © 1973, 1978, 1984, 2011 by Biblica, Inc.™ Used by permission of Zondervan. All rights reserved worldwide. www.zondervan.comThe "NIV" and "New International Version" are trademarks registered in the United States Patent and Trademark Office by Biblica, Inc.™

Scripture quotations marked ESV are from the ESV® Bible (The Holy Bible, English Standard Version®), copyright © 2001 by Crossway Bibles, a publishing ministry of Good News Publishers. Used by permission. All rights reserved.

Scripture quotations marked TPT are from The Passion Translation®. Copyright © 2017, 2018 by Passion & Fire Ministries, Inc. Used by permission. All rights reserved. ThePassionTranslation.com.

Amplified Bible (AMP) Copyright © 1954, 1958, 1962, 1964, 1965, 1987 by The Lockman Foundation, La Habra, CA. All rights reserved. Used by Permission.

Scripture quotations marked (CEV) are from the Contemporary English Version Copyright © 1991, 1992, 1995 by American Bible Society, Used by Permission.

IMAGES

Truth #01: pexels - Anna Shvets: 5067704
Truth #02: pexels - Nicole Michalou: 5778905
Truth #03: pixabay - Nathan Wright: 3395660
Truth #04: pexels - Edu Carvalho: 2050999
Truth #05: pixabay - Olya Adamovich: 2896389
Truth #06: pexels - Simon Matzinger: 1323550
Truth #07: pxhere - 945360
Truth #08: pexels - Tatiana Syrikova: 3933922
Truth #09: pexels - cottonbro: 4720389
Truth #10: pexels - Ketut Subiyanto: 4584665
Truth #11: pexels - Min An: 1629016
Truth #12: pexels - Any Lane: 5727731
Truth #13: pexels - Olya Kobruseva: 4630023
Truth #14: pixabay - Free-Photos: 768702
Truth #15: pexels - Ba Tik: 3754243
Truth #16: pxhere - stecy2001: 1604616
Truth #17: pexels - Bisesh Gurung: 2609459
Truth #18: pexels - Filipe Delgado: 1601495
Truth #19: pexels - jonas mohamadi: 1416736
Truth #20: pexels - Ikowh Babayev: 16622
Truth #21: pexels - Sarwer e Kainat Welfare: 3996734
Truth #22: pexels - TanteTati: 1156619
Truth #23: pexels - 220512
Truth #24: pexels - Andre Moura: 4796916
Truth #25: pexels - Ketut Subiyanto: 4546116
Truth #26: pexels - olia danilevich: 5088173
Truth #27: pexels - Wendy Wei: 4876309
Truth #28: pxhere - 150056
Truth #29: pexels - 70361
Truth #30: pexels - Lucas Pezeta: 3405547

CONTENTS

Introduction: Lost or Loved? 1
Truth #01: Love Always Perseveres 4
Truth #02: Love Always Provides 8
Truth #03: Love Always Pursues 12
Truth #04: Love Always Protects 16
Truth #05: Love Always Forgives 20
Truth #06: Love Is God 24
Truth #07: Love Is Permanent 28
Truth #08: Love Is Patient 32
Truth #09: Love Is Present 36
Truth #10: Love Is Vulnerable 40
Truth #11: Love Sees You 44
Truth #12: Love Favors You 48
Truth #13: Love Beautifies You 52
Truth #14: Love Comforts You 56
Truth #15: Love Understands You 60
Truth #16: Love Begets Love 64
Truth #17: Love Lasts Forever 68
Truth #18: Love Reaches You 72
Truth #19: Love Changes You 76
Truth #20: Love Perfects You 80
Truth #21: Love Overcomes Evil 84
Truth #22: Love God 88
Truth #23: Love Others 92
Truth #24: Love Your Neighbor 96
Truth #25: Love Those Who Hate You 100
Truth #26: Love Results In Action 104
Truth #27: Love Results In Freedom 108
Truth #28: Love Results In Surrender 112
Truth #29: Love Results In Boldness 116
Truth #30: Love Results In Inspiration 120

Lost or Loved?

How do you think God feels about you? Do you imagine God as welcoming you closer or ignoring you? Consider the cabin on the front cover. When its door is open, you can come inside where it's warm. But if it's locked, you must stay outside where it's cold.

Many people feel overwhelming fear as they face God's standard of perfection and then judgement. They believe God has locked the door because He is disgusted with them. They don't want to risk trying the door because finding it locked is unbearably painful.

With that kind of anticipated rejection, what can they do but wander around outside? They are lost because they believe God is not interested in looking for them.

We live in a time when virtual reality (VR) is possible. What is fantasy can seem unbelievably real. What is real can easily be lost and forgotten. VR is fun for entertainment but it's no fun when your perceived reality is a bitter cold existence apart from God.

If you've accepted Jesus Christ as your Lord and Savior... if you understand you will never be perfect by your own effort... if by faith you believe Jesus rose from the dead as a sacrifice for your sin... then not only is the door unlocked for you, but amazingly, you are already inside. You are warm, safe, and secure.

> *No one who has faith in God's Son will be condemned. But everyone who doesn't have faith in him has already been condemned for not having faith in God's only Son.*
> —John 3:18 CEV

If you are a believer, God has already searched and found you. He has already brought you home.

> *If any of you has a hundred sheep, and one of them gets lost, what will you do? Won't you leave the ninety-nine in the field and go look for the lost sheep until you find it? And when you find it, you will be so glad that you will put it on your shoulder and carry it home.*
> —Luke 15:4-6 CEV

God accepts you and cares for you. God binds your wounds. You are not lost; you are forever found. Yet, even a Christian can be deceived. Imagine you are outside, alone and cold. But actually, you are sitting inside the warm cabin convinced you are outside. You are living a nightmare by viewing life through VR goggles.

You might believe your sin is too serious or too exceptional for God to overlook even when He views you through His Jesus goggles. You might be convinced God is rejecting you, but that's one of the Deceiver's lies.

Journal Your Way To Love

You don't have to live in that reality if you put on your Jesus goggles. Then you will be able to see that you are "in" with God. Thankfulness and joy will burst forth from your heart. As you become certain of God's love, you will feel an overwhelming compassion for yourself and others.

Loving others is hard. And then sometimes loving yourself is more difficult than loving others. What if it's so challenging because, deep down, you don't believe you are lovable? Use *Journal Your Way To Love* to discover the certainty of God's love and acceptance for you.

How To Use This Book

You'll gain more from your journaling experience when you journal in layers. Journaling in layers has four steps:
1. **Represent**: communicate what is internal or subconscious by expressing it in some external or explicit medium (words, symbols, sculptures).
2. **Rest**: acknowledge what you expressed, then wait. Let it simmer, percolate, steep. Focus on something else.
3. **Review**: revisit what you expressed, taking it back in and looking for understanding and meaning.
4. **Repeat**: return to step 1.

This book has 30 truth lessons. Respond to each truth, then return at a regular interval (1 day, 1 week, or 1 month) to reflect on the truth again, including all of your previous responses. Then, write a new response. This will deepen the truth for you.

If you want more details about this method, grab a free copy of *Journal In Layers So You Can Soar Like Eagles* at ChristianConcepts.com. It's a short read and it will help you gain more from your journaling.

Love Always Perseveres

Love is patient, love is kind. It does not envy, it does not boast, it is not proud. It does not dishonor others, it is not self-seeking, it is not easily angered, it keeps no record of wrongs. Love does not delight in evil but rejoices with the truth. It always protects, always trusts, always hopes, always perseveres. Love never fails.

—1 Corinthians 13:4-8 NIV

Keep trusting in the Lord and do what is right in his eyes. Fix your heart on the promises of God and you will be secure, feasting on his faithfulness. Make God the utmost delight and pleasure of your life, and he will provide for you what you desire the most. Give God the right to direct your life, and as you trust him along the way you'll find he pulled it off perfectly!

—Psalm 37:3-5 TPT

MATT PAVLIK

In His grace He sends us times when we experience afresh the reality of His love, but in truth His love is constant, never changes and never fails.
—Ann Allfrey

And let us run with endurance the race God has set before us. We do this by keeping our eyes on Jesus, the champion who initiates and perfects our faith. Because of the joy awaiting him, he endured the cross, disregarding its shame. Now he is seated in the place of honor beside God's throne. Think of all the hostility he endured from sinful people; then you won't become weary and give up.
—Hebrews 12:1-3 NLT

Journal Your Way to Love

God, as love, never stops working to perfect you. He doesn't give up on you. There's no reason to give up on Him. Evil delights in falsehood, deception, and destruction that undermines the truth. Love seeks truth that brings healing.

God rejoices as you experience His love. It changes you, so you will feel increasingly positive about life. Even through confusing times, you will trust God by believing He is loving, according to His words. He is patient, kind, forgiving, protective, trusting, and hopeful. God never fails.

No matter what situation you are in today, even if it's worsening, God's love endures to help you finish strong. Life is guaranteed to be better, even if it takes until you reach heaven. Ask God to help you sense His unrelenting, loving grip.

Love Always Provides

Trust in the Lord with all your heart; do not depend on your own understanding. Seek his will in all you do, and he will show you which path to take.
—Proverbs 3:5-6 NLT

Would you give your child a snake if the child asked for a fish? As bad as you are, you still know how to give good gifts to your children. But your heavenly Father is even more ready to give good things to people who ask. Treat others as you want them to treat you. This is what the Law and the Prophets are all about.
—Matthew 7:10-13 CEV

MATT PAVLIK

When we come to an understanding of how much God loves us, we'll be able to truly trust Him no matter what circumstances come our way. Receive His divine love today, and release the need to control every situation. His peace will cover you.

—Kristin Reeg

There is no fear in love. But perfect love drives out fear, because fear has to do with punishment. The one who fears is not made perfect in love.

—1 John 4:18 NIV

Journal Your Way to Love

Love allows you to kick fear to the curb. Fear can grow as you expect painful, lasting consequences. But hurt doesn't have to cause you to doubt God. His trustworthiness and promises outweigh any perceived punishment or natural consequences.

God always protects, provides, and perseveres. He does not spite someone by taking something away for no good reason. Whatever you can lose isn't essential. You can thrive without it. God supplies you the opportunity to grow, be responsible, and contribute to His goals.

When you fill yourself with worry, you become a slave to fear. Are you trapped, letting your circumstances determine how you see God? Or are you living in freedom, letting God's character determine how you see your circumstances?

Love Always Pursues

The younger son got up and started back to his father. But when he was still a long way off, his father saw him and felt sorry for him. He ran to his son and hugged and kissed him. The son said, "Father, I have sinned against God in heaven and against you. I am no longer good enough to be called your son." But his father said to the servants, "Hurry and bring the best clothes and put them on him. Give him a ring for his finger and sandals for his feet. Get the best calf and prepare it, so we can eat and celebrate. This son of mine was dead, but has now come back to life. He was lost and has now been found."

—Luke 15:20-24 CEV

Behold, I'm standing at the door, knocking. If your heart is open to hear my voice and you open the door within, I will come in to you and feast with you, and you will feast with me.

—Revelation 3:20 TPT

MATT PAVLIK

God is looking for you. He'll keep pursuing you, keep calling you, keep nudging you. He loves you too much to leave you alone. He knows who you are. He breathed His life into you.

—Joel Osteen

The Lord isn't really being slow about his promise, as some people think. No, he is being patient for your sake. He does not want anyone to be destroyed, but wants everyone to repent.

—2 Peter 3:9 NLT

God pursues by looking, knocking, and waiting. He wants to celebrate with you. In order to commune with God, you must feel your neediness. Have you ever pretended that you don't need God? That's like plugging your ears when the most beautiful music is playing.

Have you ever been lost? It's easy to lose hope when you can't find your way home. Yet, when you can hear God's voice, you are never really lost. God never loses track of you.

God wants to communicate with you. But your unbelief can prevent you from hearing Him. There might also be times when God is waiting on you to return to Him or move forward in faith. Find God by separating the noise from the music. Call to Him and listen at the door of your heart. What do you hear?

Truth #04

Love Always Protects

Before I even speak a word, you know what I will say, and with your powerful arm you protect me from every side. I can't understand all of this! Such wonderful knowledge is far above me. Where could I go to escape from your Spirit or from your sight? If I were to climb up to the highest heavens, you would be there. If I were to dig down to the world of the dead you would also be there. Suppose I had wings like the dawning day and flew across the ocean. Even then your powerful arm would guide and protect me.

—Psalm 139:4-10 CEV

All of this is for your benefit. And as God's grace reaches more and more people, there will be great thanksgiving, and God will receive more and more glory. That is why we never give up. Though our bodies are dying, our spirits are being renewed every day.

—2 Corinthians 4:15-16 NLT

MATT PAVLIK

When I trust deeply that today God is truly with me and holds me safe in a divine embrace, guiding every one of my steps I can let go of my anxious need to know how tomorrow will look, or what will happen next month or next year. I can be fully where I am and pay attention to the many signs of God's love within me and around me.
—Henri J. M. Nouwen

"God's tabernacle is with human beings. And from now on he will tabernacle with them as their God. Now God himself will have his home with them—'God-with-them' will be their God! He will wipe away every tear from their eyes and eliminate death entirely. No one will mourn or weep any longer. The pain of wounds will no longer exist…"
—Romans 8:29-30 NIV

God's plan for you will be fulfilled. Jesus promises to guide you into all truth, deliver you from evil, and present you blameless before God. You can relax in His protection.

God's promises are primarily spiritual. He sustains you by healing you from the inside out. You might mourn as your body wastes away but you can rejoice because God renews your spirit, making you stronger. You might suffer now but His grace preserves you for eternity. God can transform painful experiences into powerful motivations.

You are safe in God's hands. His love shields you from evil accusations. You'll never have to worry about defending yourself. How have you experienced God's protection? What is possible to lose and what does God guarantee to protect?

Love Always Forgives

God, give me mercy from your fountain of forgiveness!
I know your abundant love is enough to wash away my guilt.
Because your compassion is so great,
take away this shameful guilt of sin.
Forgive the full extent of my rebellious ways,
and erase this deep stain on my conscience.
—Psalm 51:1-2 TPT

You were cleansed from your sins when you obeyed the truth, so now you must show sincere love to each other as brothers and sisters. Love each other deeply with all your heart.
—1 Peter 1:22 NLT

MATT PAVLIK

Parental love is unconditional, and so is God's love. No matter what a child of God has done against Him, or feels he or she has done that cannot be forgiven, God still loves that wondering soul.
—Dr. David Jeremiah

Above all, love each other deeply, because love covers over a multitude of sins. Hatred stirs up conflict, but love covers over all wrongs.
—1 Peter 4:8 NIV; Proverbs 10:12 NIV

God's fountain of forgiveness never runs dry. Guilt is relentless, especially when painful consequences linger. But thankfully, a fresh start is always possible with God. His guilt-abolishing mercies are new every morning, providing needed relief.

Jesus knows what it is like to be human, so He is the perfect person to represent you to God. His loving sacrifice covers over all wrongs. When you receive God's abundant love, you gain the power to forgive others' debt.

Hate is to will evil to another. You judge them as unworthy and condemn them. If you place your trust in God, you can let Him be the one and only true judge. If you catch yourself hating someone else, consider if you really want to wish evil upon them. Ask God to release you from hatred.

Truth #06

Love Is God

If I speak in the tongues of men or of angels, but do not have love, I am only a resounding gong or a clanging cymbal. If I have the gift of prophecy and can fathom all mysteries and all knowledge, and if I have a faith that can move mountains, but do not have love, I am nothing. If I give all I possess to the poor and give over my body to hardship that I may boast, but do not have love, I gain nothing. And now these three remain: faith, hope and love. But the greatest of these is love.

—1 Corinthians 13:1-3, 13 NIV

For my thoughts are not your thoughts, neither are your ways my ways, declares the Lord. For as the heavens are higher than the earth, so are my ways higher than your ways and my thoughts than your thoughts.

—Isaiah 55:8-9 ESV

MATT PAVLIK

*Everything God does is love --
even when we do not understand Him.*
—Basilea Schlink

And so we know and rely on the love God has for us. God is love. Whoever lives in love lives in God, and God in them. This is how love is made complete among us so that we will have confidence on the day of judgment: In this world we are like Jesus.
—1 John 4:16-17 NIV

Love makes everything work well. Nothing functions properly without it. Love enables you to know God's value and the value of the people He created. Love is a passionate, sometimes irrational, commitment to another person you value.

If it is loving, it is of God. If God does it, it is loving. Don't measure God by your idea of love. Instead, measure everything by what God says and does.

You can know God in your spirit even though you don't fully understand Him. Your understanding and knowledge are incomplete. God reveals as much of Himself as He wants you to know. You can trust God because He knows more than you ever will. You must depend on Him for everything or for nothing. What experiences have helped you to know God?

Truth #07

Love Is Permanent

But God was merciful! We were dead because of our sins, but God loved us so much that he made us alive with Christ, and God's wonderful kindness is what saves you.

—Ephesians 2:4-5 CEV

Know therefore that the Lord your God is God; he is the faithful God, keeping his covenant of love to a thousand generations of those who love him and keep his commandments.

—Deuteronomy 7:9 NIV

MATT PAVLIK

Learn to commit every situation to God, and trust Him for the outcome. God's love for you never changes, no matter what problems you face or how unsettled life becomes.
—Billy Graham

For great is your steadfast love toward me; you have delivered my soul from the depths of Sheol. O God, insolent men have risen up against me; a band of ruthless men seeks my life, and they do not set you before them. But you, O Lord, are a God merciful and gracious, slow to anger and abounding in steadfast love and faithfulness.
—Psalms 86:13-15 ESV

Journal Your Way to Love

How long would God need before He becomes tired of loving you? A thousand generations is about 25,000 years, meaning that God's love and faithfulness cannot be exhausted.

You might be kind one day and grumpy the next, but God's love is perfect and constant. God doesn't change His mind about you even when He is disciplining you. God loved you at your worst—when you were spiritually dead. But even if somehow you could be worse than God's enemy, He would not stop loving you because He sees your value.

You have value because of how God made you and who He intends for you to be. God's love for you is not dependent upon your outward behaviors. Even when you sin, He continues to think well of you and feel positively toward you.

Truth #08

Love Is Patient

Some time ago, the Lord appeared to me and told me to say: Israel, I will always love you; that's why I've been so patient and kind.

—Jeremiah 31:3 CEV

The Lord is gracious and compassionate, slow to anger and rich in love. The Lord is good to all; he has compassion on all he has made. All your works praise you, Lord; your faithful people extol you.

—Psalm 145:8-10 NIV

MATT PAVLIK

Never correct someone out of self-righteousness or a need to be right. The motive for bringing correction should be to see the other person enter into God's best for their life. Love, not pride or anger or anything else, is the driving force for biblical correction.
—John Bevere

A kind answer soothes angry feelings, but harsh words stir them up.
—Proverbs 15:1 CEV

Journal Your Way to Love

Unrighteous anger reeks of impatience. It's a cry to possess power apart from God to control fate. It's attractive because it can help you forget your pain—temporarily. But it's rooted in fear—a lack of trust in God's care and provision.

When God appears to fail to make things right, it is easy to distrust Him, shut out His influence, and determine to fulfill your will. Revenge can help you to not feel alone in your pain—temporarily. When have you felt like God has betrayed you?

A kind answer soothes pain, but a harsh word adds more hurt. Anger provides courage to speak the truth, but to be righteous, God's love must flow through you. His patience snuggles you secure in His love, empowering you to be patient. Remember when His presence has strengthened you.

Truth #09

Love Is Present

I pray that you, being rooted and established in love, may have power, together with all the Lord's holy people, to grasp how wide and long and high and deep is the love of Christ, and to know this love that surpasses knowledge—that you may be filled to the measure of all the fullness of God.

—Ephesians 3:17-19 NIV

All right then, the Lord himself will give you the sign. Look! The virgin will conceive a child! She will give birth to a son and will call him Immanuel (which means 'God is with us').

—Isaiah 7:14 NLT

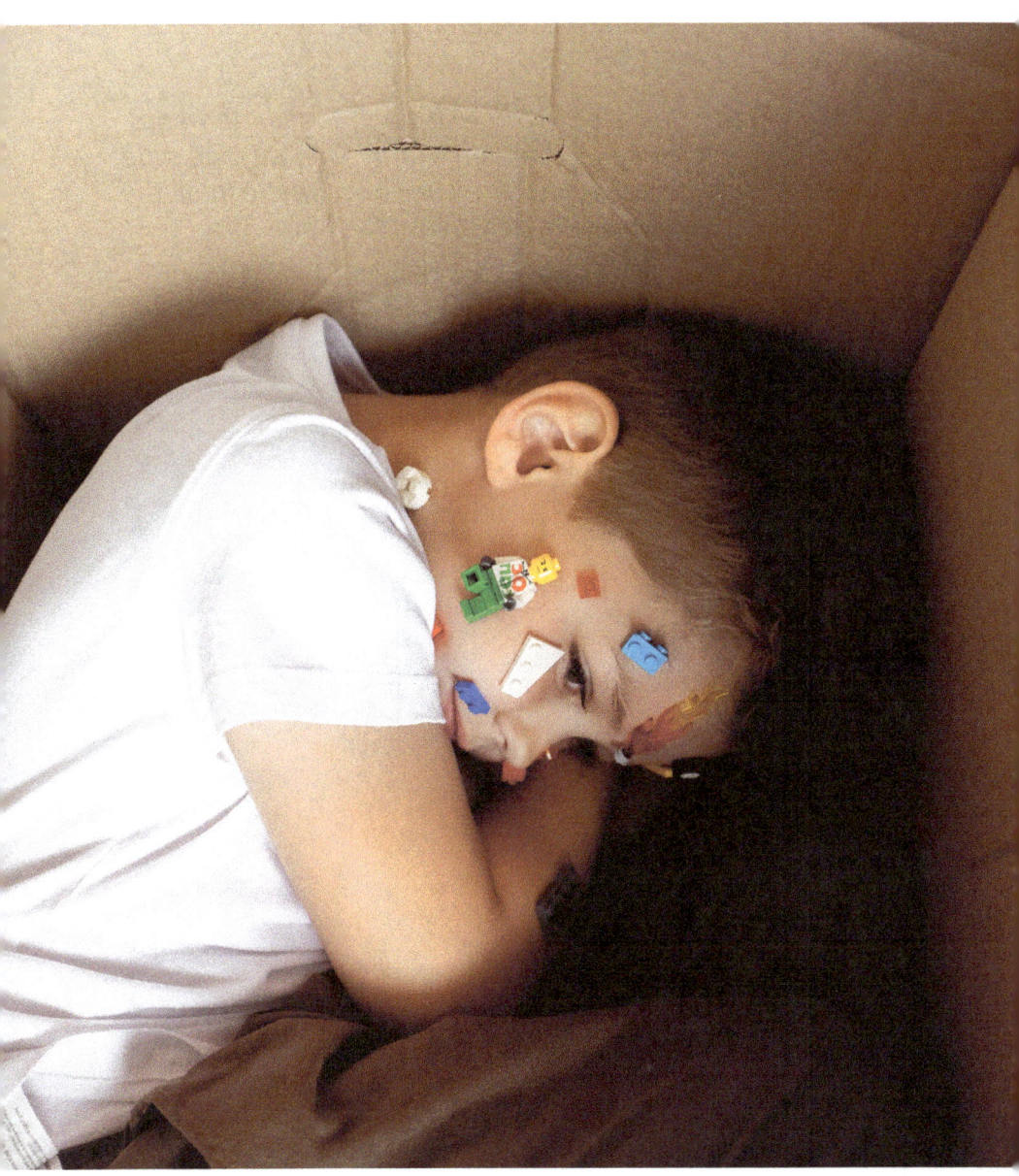

MATT PAVLIK

*Jesus healed people one at a time
because God cares about individual people.*
—John MacArthur (edited)

Am I a God who is only close at hand?" says the Lord. "No, I am far away at the same time. Can anyone hide from me in a secret place? Am I not everywhere in all the heavens and earth?" says the Lord.
—Jeremiah 23:23-24 NLT

Journal Your Way to Love

Love surpasses everyday knowledge. It's impossible to fully understand the depth and breadth of God's love without the help of the Holy Spirit who provides powerful spiritual insight.

God's love is global. He is everywhere. You can't run away from God. You can't hide from God. Even if you ran as far away as you can, God would still be there with you (Psalm 139).

God's love is universal, but it's also personal. His love is more than mere talk. It's action. God cared enough to become like one of us. Jesus is our Immanuel, God with us. He holds together the partnership between God and humanity. Whether you are joyful or depressed, secure or lonely, Jesus is there. Activate your faith. Believe Jesus is right there with you. Tell Him how you are doing.

Love Is Vulnerable

Three times I begged the Lord to make this suffering go away. But he replied, "My kindness is all you need. My power is strongest when you are weak."
—2 Corinthians 12:8-9 CEV

Mary went to where Jesus was. Then as soon as she saw him, she knelt at his feet and said, "Lord, if you had been here, my brother would not have died." Jesus started crying, and the people said, "See how much he loved Lazarus." Jesus was still terribly upset. So he went to the tomb, which was a cave with a stone rolled against the entrance. Then he told the people to roll the stone away. After the stone had been rolled aside, Jesus looked up toward heaven and prayed, "Father, I thank you for answering my prayer. When Jesus had finished praying, he shouted, "Lazarus, come out!"
—John 11:34-36, 38-39, 41, 43 CEV

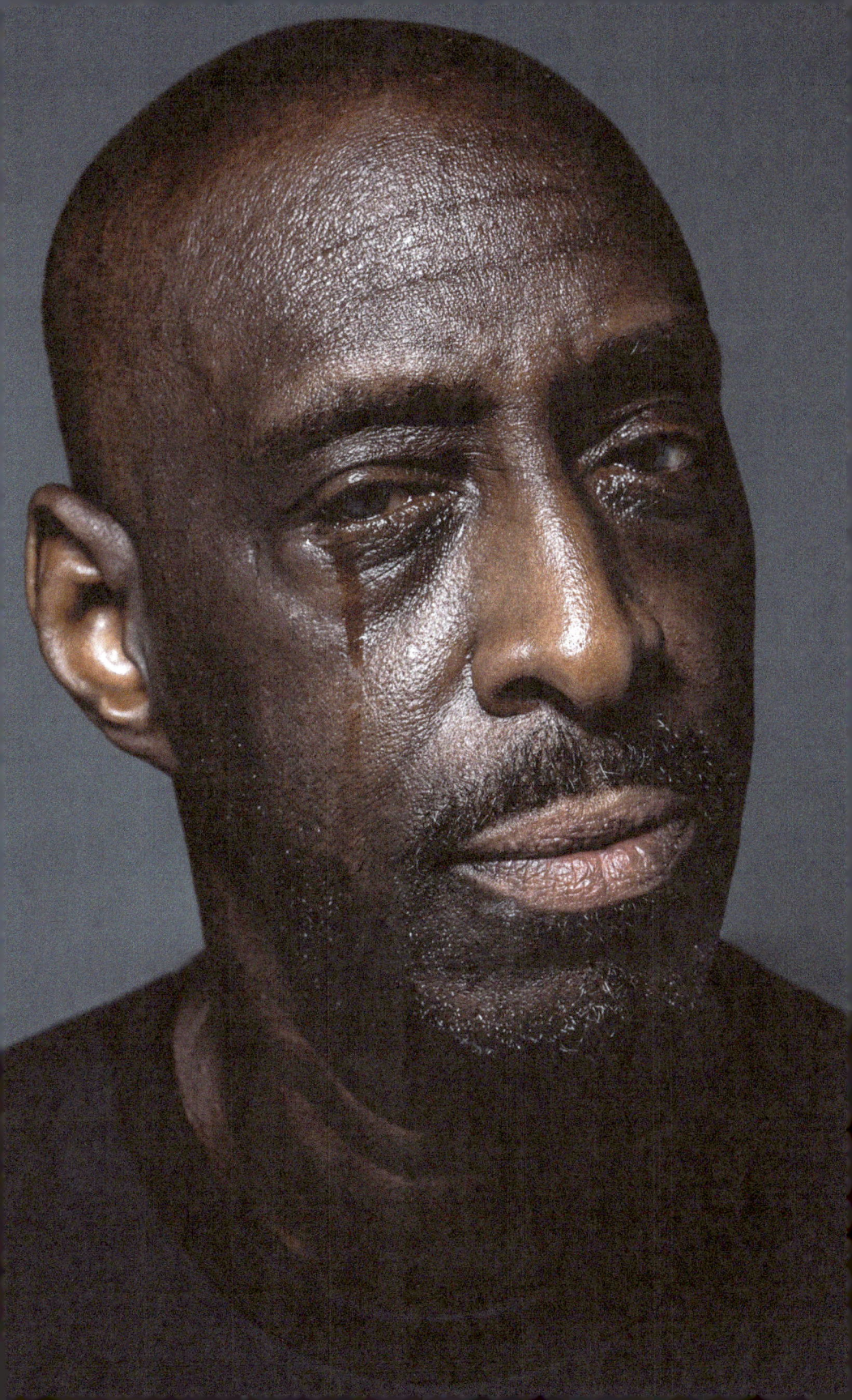

MATT PAVLIK

To love at all is to be vulnerable. Love anything and your heart will be wrung and possibly broken. If you want to make sure of keeping it intact you must give it to no one. Wrap it carefully round with hobbies and little luxuries; avoid all entanglements. Lock it up safe in the casket or coffin of your selfishness. But in that casket, safe, dark, motionless, airless, it will change. It will not be broken; it will become unbreakable, impenetrable, irredeemable.

—C.S. Lewis (edited)

For God so loved the world that he gave his one and only Son, that whoever believes in him shall not perish but have eternal life.

—John 3:16 NIV

Journal Your Way to Love

When are you most likely to feel deep sorrow? How about when you see the many ways you and others fall short of God's love? But all is not lost. In humility, you can hunger for the truth and righteousness.

Human weakness, vulnerability, and openness allow God to strengthen you. God becoming human and sacrificing Himself was a vulnerable act. His love is strong and caring. When you respond to His love with openness, you become strong, vulnerable, and caring.

Caring for others costs you. But, you will gladly bear hardship if it benefits the person you love. Caring gives you the motivation to sacrifice. What are your thoughts on, "Tis better to have loved and lost than never loved at all" (Tennyson)?

Love Sees You

You have looked deep into my heart, Lord, and you know all about me. You know when I am resting or when I am working, and from heaven you discover my thoughts. You notice everything I do and everywhere I go. Before I even speak a word, you know what I will say.

—Psalm 139:1-4 CEV

Truthful lips endure forever, but a lying tongue lasts only a moment. The tongue of the wise adorns knowledge, but the mouth of the fool gushes folly. The eyes of the LORD are everywhere, keeping watch on the wicked and the good.

—Proverbs 12:19, 15:2-3 NIV

MATT PAVLIK

To love someone means to see him as God intended him.
—Fyodor Dostoevsky

God shows his love for us in that while we were still sinners, Christ died for us.
—Romans 5:8 ESV

Love sees everything; it isn't blind. Love isn't love without the truth. God sees you at your worst and never loses sight of who you are at your best. He chose you knowing what your worst would cost Him. God focuses on your real self, the one He intended, not your defects. Your defects are temporary while your best qualities are forever. What is false isn't real because it has no place in eternity.

Sin is a disease that causes a person to reject God—reject the highest of standards. When you reject God, you also reject yourself. What parts of you are you rejecting?

You can only love yourself by seeing yourself as God sees you. Then you'll also be able to see and admire others the way God does. What parts of you are going to last forever?

Love Favors You

Before the world was created, God had Christ choose us to live with him and to be his holy and innocent and loving people. God was kind and decided that Christ would choose us to be God's own adopted children.
—Ephesians 1:4-5 CEV

Dear brothers and sisters, you are dearly loved by God and we know that he has chosen you to be his very own.
—1 Thessalonians 1:4 TPT

Many are invited, but only a few are chosen.
—Matthew 22:14 CEV

MATT PAVLIK

It is time to really not only believe but to know that all things are possible with God and you are His favorite. You are blessed and highly favored, deeply loved and just right!

—Bob Richardson

Israel, I, the Lord, have loved you. And yet you ask in what way have I loved you. Don't forget that Esau was the brother of your ancestor Jacob, but I chose Jacob instead of Esau.

—Malachi 1:2-3 CEV

Journal Your Way to Love

To be favored means to be singled out from other options. God chooses a family of believers while excluding unbelievers. There is a reason God chose you. Let this sink in.

You can be favored by God even when others are too. God has an infinite supply of love. God's relationship with you is unique so His favor rests on you like no other. As God's chosen, you are not stealing someone else's spot, nor can anyone steal your place with Him.

You can embrace your favored status without guilt. You are not superior to others, but you are valued, important, and needed. You have no competition for being you. Sharing the joy of being chosen might help others find their desire to know a favored status.

Love Beautifies You

I have seen the burden God has placed on us all. Yet God has made everything beautiful for its own time. He has planted eternity in the human heart, but even so, people cannot see the whole scope of God's work from beginning to end. So I concluded there is nothing better than to be happy and enjoy ourselves as long as we can.

—Ecclesiastes 3:10-12 NLT

To all who mourn in Israel, he will give a crown of beauty for ashes, a joyous blessing instead of mourning, festive praise instead of despair. In their righteousness, they will be like great oaks that the Lord has planted for his own glory.

—Isaiah 61:3 NLT

MATT PAVLIK

*Since love grows within you, so beauty grows.
For love is the beauty of the soul.*
—Augustine

Let your true beauty come from your inner personality, not a focus on the external. For lasting beauty comes from a gentle and peaceful spirit, which is precious in God's sight and is much more important than the outward adornment of elaborate hair, jewelry, and fine clothes.
—1 Peter 3:3-4 TPT

No one is responsible for knowing everything that God is trying to accomplish. Beauty frees you up to enjoy life because encountering it brings you in touch with eternity. Whatever is beautiful will last forever. You can't enjoy all of the beauty right now, but you can taste portions of its fruit.

Beauty includes not only what is pleasing to the eye, but also what is pleasing to the mind. Both men and women are beautiful. Tend to your outward beauty but focus on your inward beauty. Since you are made in His image to last forever, you are wonderful and captivating.

Does a part of you seem broken or ugly? God is restoring you by drawing the beauty of your spirit to the surface. Ask God to help you experience His healing touch.

Love Comforts You

Get wisdom, get understanding; do not forget my words or turn away from them. Do not forsake wisdom, and she will protect you; love her, and she will watch over you.

How much better to get wisdom than gold,
to get insight rather than silver!

—Proverbs 4:5-6, 16:16 NIV

Don't be obsessed with money but live content with what you have, for you always have God's presence. For hasn't he promised you, "I will never leave you alone, never! And I will not loosen my grip on your life!"

—Hebrews 13:5 TPT

MATT PAVLIK

God doesn't owe us an explanation for everything and actually what I've found is that explanations don't comfort. What comforts is the presence of God, not the explanation of God.
—Rick Warren

Praise God, the Father of our Lord Jesus Christ! The Father is a merciful God, who always gives us comfort. He comforts us when we are in trouble, so that we can share that same comfort with others in trouble. We share in the terrible sufferings of Christ, but also in the wonderful comfort he gives.
—2 Corinthians 1:3-5 CEV

Journal Your Way to Love

Loneliness results when you lose track of God's loving presence. Like leprosy in the body, loneliness causes your soul to wither. If you are closed off to God, you will always feel lonely no matter how many people are around. Anxiety comes from a lack of connection with God, whether actual (for unbeliever) or perceived (for believer).

When you sense God's presence with you, that is supreme comfort. You can endure being apart from others when you know God will never reject you. He is always with you and for you. His presence is worth more than any amount of money.

When you open to God, His Spirit of wisdom grants you security, vibrancy, and comfort. Notice how open or closed you are to God and how much peace and comfort you have.

Love Understands You

*A fool takes no pleasure in understanding,
but only in expressing his opinion.*

*Before destruction a man's heart is haughty,
but humility comes before honor.*

*If one gives an answer before he hears,
it is his folly and shame.*

—Proverbs 18:2, 12-13 ESV

*My child, listen to what I say,
and treasure my commands.*

*Tune your ears to wisdom,
and concentrate on understanding.*

*Cry out for insight,
and ask for understanding.*

—Proverbs 2:1-3 NLT

MATT PAVLIK

*One of the best ways to demonstrate
God's love is to listen to people.*
—Bruce Larsen

*The purpose in a man's heart is like deep water,
but a man of understanding will draw it out.*
—Proverbs 20:5 ESV

*Each heart knows its own bitterness,
and no one else can fully share its joy.*
—Proverbs 14:10 NLT

Communication can be like two people trying to find each other in the dark. To be successful, the speaker must assist the listener. "I'm over here. Am I making sense? I don't feel understood yet. Keep trying."

Listening requires effort because only God fully knows each person. Knowing your own heartache helps you identify more completely with others. The best listening leads to appreciation, even if you never reach agreement.

You will feel most loved when someone else understands and accepts you. But misunderstanding fuels confusion and loneliness. Your heart has a language that can express who you are and the condition of your soul. Do you want to be found, or do you prefer to play hide-and-seek?

Love Begets Love

Then turning toward the woman he said to Simon, "Do you see this woman? I entered your house; you gave me no water for my feet, but she has wet my feet with her tears and wiped them with her hair. You gave me no kiss, but from the time I came in she has not ceased to kiss my feet. You did not anoint my head with oil, but she has anointed my feet with ointment. Therefore I tell you, her sins, which are many, are forgiven—for she loved much. But he who is forgiven little, loves little."
—Luke 7:44-47 ESV

We love because he first loved us.
—1 John 4:19 ESV

MATT PAVLIK

When you realize that you are deeply loved by God, it enables you to love deeply.
—Marty Cauley

The Pharisees and some of their teachers of the Law of Moses grumbled to Jesus' disciples, "Why do you eat and drink with those tax collectors and other sinners?" Jesus answered, "Healthy people don't need a doctor, but sick people do. I didn't come to invite good people to turn to God. I came to invite sinners."
—Luke 5:30-32 CEV

Journal Your Way to Love

Everyone is sick with sin but not everyone realizes the disease is fatal. The more you understand its seriousness, the more likely you are to visit the great Physician, Jesus Christ.

Being aware of your brokenness enables you to be aware of God's wholeness. God's healing touch and acceptance always change you for the better. You can understand that no one owes you anything. Gratitude and compassion will burst forth from your heart empowering you to forgive others.

God invites those who can genuinely appreciate what He has done for them. When you realize how much God has forgiven in you, you won't take it for granted. You experience God's love; then you respond with thankfulness. God's love enables you to exchange guilt for gratitude.

Love Lasts Forever

Give thanks to the Lord, for he is good!
His faithful love endures forever.
Give thanks to him who alone does mighty miracles.
His faithful love endures forever.

Give thanks to him who led
his people through the wilderness.
His faithful love endures forever.
Give thanks to him who struck down mighty kings.
His faithful love endures forever.

He remembered us in our weakness.
His faithful love endures forever.
He saved us from our enemies.
His faithful love endures forever.

—Psalm 136:1, 4, 16, 17, 23, 24 NLT

MATT PAVLIK

God is completely sovereign. God is infinite in wisdom. God is perfect in love. God in His love always wills what is best for us. In His wisdom He always knows what is best, and in His sovereignty He has the power to bring it about.
—Jerry Bridges

God knew his people in advance, and he chose them to become like his Son, so that his Son would be the firstborn among many brothers and sisters. And having chosen them, he called them to come to him. And having called them, he gave them right standing with himself. And having given them right standing, he gave them his glory.
—Romans 8:29-30 NLT

Journal Your Way to Love

God's plan and purpose are inevitable. His plan includes seeing you become complete. His love doesn't have a reverse gear or a throttle—it's always full speed ahead. What aspects of your life do you believe will survive into eternity?

Pray for what seems like the best outcome, but be prepared to accept God's decision. If God wants something to change, He can bring the change. The Israelites suffered 400 years before God took action. Everything He does has a reason.

Pray with persistence but understand God will respond in the right way at the right time. When He doesn't respond, it's not the right time. When He does respond, you can trust it is the right time. You can live with more certainty about your future. Meditate on, *His faithful love endures forever.*

Love Reaches You

God's Spirit makes us loving, happy, peaceful, patient, kind, good, faithful, gentle, and self-controlled. There is no law against behaving in any of these ways.

—Galatians 5:22-23 CEV

I pray that you, being rooted and established in love, may have power, together with all the Lord's holy people, to grasp how wide and long and high and deep is the love of Christ, and to know this love that surpasses knowledge— that you may be filled to the measure of all the fullness of God.

—Ephesians 3:17-19 NIV

MATT PAVLIK

There is no pit so deep, that God's love is not deeper still.
—Corrie Ten Boom

God's law was given so that all people could see how sinful they were. But as people sinned more and more, God's wonderful grace became more abundant.
—Romans 5:20 NLT

Journal Your Way to Love

However big your need, God's love is up to the task. Love doesn't run out or fall short. God is able to abundantly supply you with the fruit of His Spirit. The more you exercise your heart by practicing His love, the more energy you have to love.

How can the fullness of God, who is infinite, dwell in your heart? God's power stretches your heart, so it can hold His love. God's love and grace can also stretch to be as big as needed to cover your sin.

God's arm is long enough to reach you wherever you are. However deep your pit, God is right there with you. He comes to you because you can't reach Him on your own. What challenges do you face at the bottom of your pit? Ask God for more insight into the depths of His love.

Love Changes You

"I am the true grapevine, and my Father is the gardener. He cuts off every branch of mine that doesn't produce fruit, and he prunes the branches that do bear fruit so they will produce even more. You have already been pruned and purified by the message I have given you. Remain in me, and I will remain in you. For a branch cannot produce fruit if it is severed from the vine, and you cannot be fruitful unless you remain in me."

—John 15:1-4 NLT

Beloved, we are God's children now, and what we will be has not yet appeared; but we know that when he appears we shall be like him, because we shall see him as he is. And everyone who thus hopes in him purifies himself as he is pure.

—1 John 3:2-3 ESV

MATT PAVLIK

As you begin to love others as you love yourself and strive to do unto others as you would have others do unto you, you will find that you are changing, and that change comes from the heart by the indwelling Holy Spirit.
—Gaines Johnson

And may the Lord make your love for one another and for all people grow and overflow, just as our love for you overflows.
—1 Thessalonians 3:12 NLT

A sapling cannot stay two feet tall. It's meant to become a full-grown tree. Don't love the sapling so much that you smother it to death. Anything alive is meant to grow and become all that God means for it to be. Don't love yourself so much that when God prunes you, you no longer recognize who you are. Accept pruning as God's sovereign direction for your life.

Once anything stops changing, it's truly dead. As long as you can sense the smallest amount of growth, you can evict your fear and keep hope alive.

What do you notice is different about you in the past year? How has God purified and pruned you? What are your best opportunities for growth? Practice being hopeful. Notice how pure and free you feel.

Love Perfects You

And above all these put on love, which binds everything together in perfect harmony.
—Colossians 3:14 ESV

Don't copy the behavior and customs of this world, but let God transform you into a new person by changing the way you think. Then you will learn to know God's will for you, which is good and pleasing and perfect.
—Romans 12:2 NLT

It's not about finding ways to avoid God's judgment and feeling like a failure if you don't do everything perfectly. It's about fully experiencing God's love and letting it perfect you. It's not about being somebody you are not. It's about becoming who you really are.

—Stormie Omartian

Now all we can see of God is like a cloudy picture in a mirror. Later we will see him face to face. We don't know everything, but then we will, just as God completely understands us.

—1 Corinthians 13:12 CEV

Journal Your Way to Love

When you stubbornly hold on to old ways of thinking, you delay God's work to perfect you. His creative design for you doesn't need to change. You have Christ's full acceptance as He corrects your defects. You will attain a whole new level of perfection later, when God calls you home to heaven.

Loving others is the hardest thing you'll ever have to do. God's standards are the highest possible. But once you let God be in control, His power renews your mind and you'll find loving others is easier.

As you become closer to God, you become the real, perfect you. You don't feel ashamed of who you are, even when you struggle with sin. How well are you knowing and becoming who you really are? At knowing God's perfect will for you?

Truth #21

Love Overcomes Evil

Love must be sincere. Hate what is evil; cling to what is good. Be devoted to one another in love. Honor one another above yourselves.

—Romans 12:9-10 NIV

On the contrary: "If your enemy is hungry, feed him; if he is thirsty, give him something to drink. In doing this, you will heap burning coals on his head." Do not be overcome by evil, but overcome evil with good."

—Romans 12:20-21 NIV

MATT PAVLIK

Darkness cannot drive out darkness: only light can do that. Hate cannot drive out hate: only love can do that.
—Martin Luther King Jr.

Even though it is written: All day long we face death threats for your sake, God. We are considered to be nothing more than sheep to be slaughtered! Yet even in the midst of all these things, we triumph over them all, for God has made us to be more than conquerors, and his demonstrated love is our glorious victory over everything!
—Romans 8:36-37 TPT

When God says to love your enemy, He is asking you to care about a fellow human. The spiritual power of evil is your true enemy. God isn't saying to love evil. You can win over a person through love because love has power to defeat evil.

It is impossible to love an under-the-influence-of-evil person without an unwavering, firm belief in God. Loving your enemy is only possible as you draw strength from God. Without God's strength you will inevitably retreat into your own human selfishness. You will prioritize self-preservation.

God's love is real and has the power to overcome evil's darkness. Don't try to love others with only your love. You must love using God's love. Can you think of someone you are struggling to love? Ask God for His love.

Love God

"Teacher, what is the most important commandment in the Law?" Jesus answered: Love the Lord your God with all your heart, soul, and mind. This is the first and most important commandment.
—Matthew 22:36-38 CEV

He said to another man, "Follow me." But he replied, "Lord, first let me go and bury my father." Jesus said to him, "Let the dead bury their own dead, but you go and proclaim the kingdom of God." Still another said, "I will follow you, Lord; but first let me go back and say goodbye to my family." Jesus replied, "No one who puts a hand to the plow and looks back is fit for service in the kingdom of God."
—Luke 9:59-62 NIV

MATT PAVLIK

*Faith makes all things possible.
Love makes all things easy.*
—Paulo Coelho

A large crowd was following Jesus. He turned around and said to them, "If you want to be my disciple, you must, by comparison, hate everyone else—your father and mother, wife and children, brothers and sisters—yes, even your own life. Otherwise, you cannot be my disciple.
—Luke 14:25-26 NLT

Journal Your Way to Love

God asks you to give your all, then He provides everything you need to make life work. His loyal love overlooks faults, sees value, and works for your good.

It's faith that makes loving God and others possible. Then it is easier to accept life's difficulties, whether they come directly or indirectly from God's hand. Without faith, you might choose to love creation more than your Creator. Even when it seems like God is against you, He is your only hope. Success means living without giving up hope.

God's love for you makes it possible to be incomplete and stand in His presence. In return, God asks for your genuine loving devotion. Put Him first and don't hold anything back from Him. How ready are you to give your all to God?

Love Others

The second most important commandment is like this one. And it is, "Love others as much as you love yourself."
—Matthew 22:39 CEV

A new commandment I give to you, that you love one another: just as I have loved you, you also are to love one another. By this all people will know that you are my disciples, if you have love for one another.
—John 13:34-35 ESV

MATT PAVLIK

Love, not anger, brought Jesus to the cross. Golgotha came as a result of God's great desire to forgive, not his reluctance. Jesus knew that by his vicarious suffering he could actually absorb all the evil of humanity and so heal it, forgive it, redeem it.

—Richard J. Foster

My command is this: Love each other as I have loved you. Greater love has no one than this: to lay down one's life for one's friends. You are my friends if you do what I command.

—John 15:12-14 NIV

Journal Your Way to Love

Some people don't know how to take care of themselves. How can they care for others? Self-care includes proper rest and nutrition. It means being kind to yourself, liking yourself, and allowing yourself to enjoy the life God has given to you.

God desires that you love others as much as you love yourself. As you become skilled in self-care, you increase your ability to put yourself in another person's shoes and sense how to love and care for them.

The more you know contentment, the easier it is to lay down your life to help others find peace. Learn what you need and what you don't. Learn what is best for you and what will be harmful. How much are you invested in self-care or self-harm? Where is your self-care lacking?

Truth #24

Love Your Neighbor

But he, desiring to justify himself, said to Jesus, "And who is my neighbor?" Jesus replied, "A man was going down from Jerusalem to Jericho, and he fell among robbers, who stripped him and beat him and departed, leaving him half dead. Now by chance a priest was going down that road, and when he saw him he passed by on the other side. So likewise a Levite, when he came to the place and saw him, passed by on the other side. But a Samaritan, as he journeyed, came to where he was, and when he saw him, he had compassion. He went to him and bound up his wounds, pouring on oil and wine. Then he set him on his own animal and brought him to an inn and took care of him.

—Luke 10:29-34 ESV

MATT PAVLIK

*Jesus loved people others rejected-
even people who rejected him. This is how God loves.*
—Gregory A. Boyd

This is how God showed his love among us: He sent his one and only Son into the world that we might live through him. This is love: not that we loved God, but that he loved us and sent his Son as an atoning sacrifice for our sins. Dear friends, since God so loved us, we also ought to love one another. No one has ever seen God; but if we love one another, God lives in us and his love is made complete in us.
—1 John 4:9-12 NIV

Your neighbor can be family or someone you just met—anyone you are aware of having a legitimate need. Being a blessing is more than satisfying a physical need or helping someone out of trouble. A blessing makes a significant spiritual contribution. Who is your neighbor?

Genuine love overflows from one life to another. A deep emotional wound like rejection can create fear that blocks the flow of love. To develop a steady flow of love for others, you must invest time to receive God's healing love and acceptance.

God expects believers to hold a special affection for other believers. Believers are part of the same spiritual family; we are brothers and sisters in Christ. God has special plans for everyone who will spend eternity together.

Love Those Who Hate You

But to you who are listening I say: Love your enemies, do good to those who hate you, bless those who curse you, pray for those who mistreat you. If someone slaps you on one cheek, turn to them the other also. If someone takes your coat, do not withhold your shirt from them. Give to everyone who asks you, and if anyone takes what belongs to you, do not demand it back. Do to others as you would have them do to you.

—Luke 6:27-31 NIV

But love your enemies, do good to them, and lend to them without expecting to get anything back. Then your reward will be great, and you will be children of the Most High, because he is kind to the ungrateful and wicked.

—Luke 6:35 NIV

MATT PAVLIK

*You will never really love until
you love someone who hates you.*
—Jack Hyles

But those who won't care for their relatives, especially those in their own household, have denied the true faith. Such people are worse than unbelievers.
— 1 Timothy 5:8 NLT

*Train up a child in the way he should go;
even when he is old he will not depart from it.*
—Proverbs 22:6 ESV

Journal Your Way To Love

Sometimes it's harder to love the "enemy" who is a member of your family. When a stranger mistreats you, it isn't as personal. But a person you care about has more power to hurt you. Evil, your true enemy, desires to turn people against each other.

Even though immature people can mistreat you, God expects you to continue to do what is best for them. As you love those who hate you, you will experience God's love in a special way— you will become secure and confident. Such a supernatural love can't come from you.

God is kind to those who don't have a clue how to love. He wants you to be able to love like He does. Love must come from God, from strength, or it isn't real love. Ask God to help you grow in your capacity to love so that others will know Him.

Truth #26

Love Results In Action

Dear friends, since God so loved us, we also ought to love one another.
And he has given us this command: Anyone who loves God must also love their brother and sister.
—1 John 4:11, 21 NIV

Do everything in love.
—1 Corinthians 16:14 NIV

If the world hates you, remember that it hated me first.
—John 15:18 NLT

In the New Testament, love is more of a verb than a noun. It has more to do with acting than with feeling. The call to love is not so much a call to a certain state of feeling as it is to a quality of action.

—R. C. Sproul

This is how we know what love is: Jesus Christ laid down his life for us. And we ought to lay down our lives for our brothers and sisters. If anyone has material possessions and sees a brother or sister in need but has no pity on them, how can the love of God be in that person? Dear children, let us not love with words or speech but with actions and in truth.

—1 John 3:16-18 NIV

Journal Your Way to Love

Words alone aren't much of a risk. But a sacrificial act is risky. Some people can't tolerate real love. They will reject you even when you show them genuine, life-giving love.

God's love working in you will move you out of your comfort zone and into some kind of helpful activity. When you're ready to act, consider whether your intentions will help or harm the person in the long run. God lets difficulty mature you. Likewise, you can allow another's pain to mature them.

Each life is precious. You are just as important as anyone else. God doesn't ask you to devalue yourself; He asks you to consider others worth serving. Serving others won't prevent bad things from happening to you. Yet, how wonderful it is to value others so much that you'd lay down your life for them.

Love Results In Freedom

Christ has set us free! This means we are really free. Now hold on to your freedom and don't ever become slaves of the Law again.

—Galatians 5:1 CEV

My friends, you were chosen to be free. So don't use your freedom as an excuse to do anything you want. Use it as an opportunity to serve each other with love.

—Galatians 5:13 CEV

MATT PAVLIK

Right after establishing that God must be first, we are reminded that God should be in this position out of love, not out of duty.
—Mark J Musser

*Now the Lord is the Spirit,
and where the Spirit of the Lord is,
there is freedom.*
—2 Corinthians 3:17 NIV

To be truly free brings great joy to life. The best love, the love God offers, comes with freedom. Obligation hinders a loving connection because it focuses on debt repayment. God's self-sufficiency and cancellation of your debt allows freedom and loyal devotion to coexist.

Obligation isn't in God's vocabulary and it shouldn't be in yours. God loves because it's His nature to do so. He can't not love. He expresses love with ease—it's never forced. Without God, actions might look like love, but they are a counterfeit.

Without freedom, motives become tainted. Are you acting because you want to or because you feel you have no other choice? Absolute freedom allows you to see your true motives. How would more freedom change your life?

Love Results In Surrender

When Jesus saw the large crowd coming toward him, he asked Philip, "Where will we get enough food to feed all these people?" He said this to test Philip, since he already knew what he was going to do. Philip answered, "Don't you know that it would take almost a year's wages just to buy only a little bread for each of these people?" Andrew, the brother of Simon Peter, was one of the disciples. He spoke up and said, "There is a boy here who has five small loaves of barley bread and two fish."

—John 6:5-9 CEV

A poor widow came and dropped in two small coins. Jesus called his disciples to him and said, "I tell you the truth, this poor widow has given more than all the others who are making contributions. For they gave a tiny part of their surplus, but she, poor as she is, has given everything she had to live on."

—Mark 12:42-44 NLT

MATT PAVLIK

Do not think that love in order to be genuine has to be extraordinary. What we need is to love without getting tired. Be faithful in small things because it is in them that your strength lies.

—Mother Teresa

"The master was full of praise. 'Well done, my good and faithful servant. You have been faithful in handling this small amount, so now I will give you many more responsibilities. Let's celebrate together!'

—Matthew 25:21 NLT

Journal Your Way to Love

God's love provides the security you need to fully surrender. When you're secure in God's love, the size of your surrender matters more than the size of your contribution. A surrendered person gives all they have and has no need for comparison.

God multiplies even your smallest contributions. He knows how to accomplish His purpose no matter how much you have. God sees everyone's heart. He rewards based on openness of heart rather than size of accomplishment. A willing heart gives its all to accomplish great things for God.

When you surrender, you give up the notion that you are self-sufficient. God is the one who makes you sufficient. Does anything hold you back from giving your all to God? How have you seen God multiply what you offer to Him?

Truth #29

Love Results In Boldness

For two whole years Paul stayed there in his own rented house and welcomed all who came to see him. He proclaimed the kingdom of God and taught about the Lord Jesus Christ—with all boldness and without hindrance!
—Acts 28:30-31 NIV

Never doubt God's mighty power to work in you and accomplish all this. He will achieve infinitely more than your greatest request, your most unbelievable dream, and exceed your wildest imagination! He will outdo them all, for his miraculous power constantly energizes you.
—Ephesians 3:20 TPT

MATT PAVLIK

If God is your partner, make your plans BIG!
—D.L. Moody

I've commanded you to be strong and brave. Don't ever be afraid or discouraged! I am the Lord your God, and I will be there to help you wherever you go.
—Joshua 1:9 CEV

Can anyone really harm you for being eager to do good deeds? Even if you have to suffer for doing good things, God will bless you. So stop being afraid and don't worry about what people might do.
—1 Peter 3:12-14 NLT

JOURNAL YOUR WAY TO LOVE

As you receive God's love, your confidence and faith increase to all-time highs. That's where God wants you. A partnership between you and God means you both give your all to the same goal. Faith allows you to receive big dreams from God and ultimately accomplish great things for Him.

Remind yourself, daily if necessary, that it's good to be confident in your faith in God. When you act on your boldness, you might find you have room to grow. This can be humbling, but learning from your mistakes generates more confidence.

If you're eager to act like God, then what is there to stop you? Don't ever stop trying. Align your heart with the right motive as you seek God's kingdom and your plans will succeed. God has specific plans for you that require your boldness.

Truth #30

Love Results In Inspiration

You bless those people who are honest and fair in everything they do. Remember me, Lord, when you show kindness by saving your people. Let me prosper with the rest of your chosen ones, as they celebrate with pride because they belong to you.
—Psalm 106:3-5 CEV

For God will never give you the spirit of fear, but the Holy Spirit who gives you mighty power, love, and self-control.
—2 Timothy 1:7 TPT

*Life is too short, the world is too big,
and God's love it too great to live ordinary.*
—Christine Caine

*Do you see any truly competent workers? They will serve
kings rather than working for ordinary people.*
—Proverbs 22:29 NLT

Journal Your Way to Love

God's love is a creative, contagious affection. You have the power to be creative, to focus, and to accomplish great works. The moment you act changes everything. Each step forward, each educated risk, is a significant, creative act.

God is creative—He made multitudes of people to display His love in as many different ways. He is capable of doing a new work in you and through you every day.

To be inspired is to be filled with the Holy Spirit. Ask God to help you be in tune with His Spirit. Ask for mighty power to accomplish spiritual work. Ask to be passionate and loving in the way you work. Ask for patience and self-control to follow the best path at the best pace. Ask for new thinking, new inspiration, and new hope.

JOURNAL IN LAYERS

Now that you have completed the first pass through these truths, remember to revisit them and your writing to gain the full benefit. You might be amazed at what you understood at first. But you can learn more with each pass you make.

To gain the most from journaling, here are some other journal-in-layers techniques to try:

- Return at a regular interval to follow up with your previous entry. This is the secret to developing deeper truth in your heart.
- Limit the number of truths you explore in each layer. For example, focus on the first seven truths in a week. Revisit them each week for four weeks. Or, if God is speaking to you through one particular truth, focus on it for several days.
- Focus on only one scripture at a time. Review one verse from each lesson, then journal another layer.
- Focus on the lesson's quote or picture.
- Draw your own picture that represents the truth.
- Write your own prayer in response to the lesson.
- Focus on one particular emotion you feel as you read the lesson. Write about that feeling and other times you've felt that way.
- Focus on the past if you need healing. Focus on the present if you feel anxious. Focus on the future if you feel restless.

Have you tried another technique that works for you? Would you like to share how has this book been a blessing to you? Contact me at mpavlik@christianconcepts.com. You can learn more about journaling by getting *Soar Like Eagles* at ChristianConcepts.com.

ABOUT MATT PAVLIK

Matt Pavlik is a licensed professional clinical counselor who wants each individual restored to their true identity. He completed his Masters in Clinical Pastoral Counseling from Ashland Theological Seminary and his Bachelors in Computer Science from the University of Illinois.

He's been a Christian since 1991 and started journaling around that time. Matt and his wife Georgette have been married since 1999 and live with their four children in Centerville, Ohio.

Blogger

Learn more at ChristianConcepts.com.

Professional Counselor

Matt has more than 15 years of experience counseling individuals and couples at his Christian private practice, New Reflections Counseling (NewReflectionsCounseling.com).

Author

Matt has written over five books on Christian identity, marriage, and spiritual life. Visit ChristianConcepts.com, ToIdentityAndBeyond.com, ConfidentIdentity.com, and MarriageFromRootsToFruits.com for details.

Identity and Marriage Books

  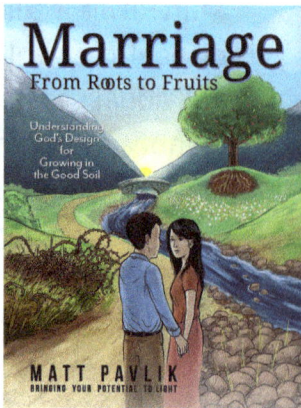

Journal Your Way Books

  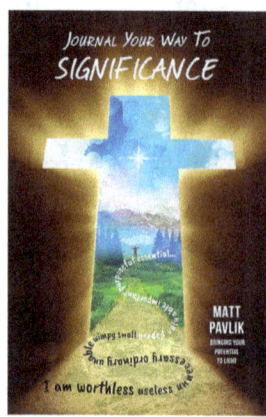

www.ingramcontent.com/pod-product-compliance
Lightning Source LLC
Chambersburg PA
CBHW050408130526
44592CB00047B/1453